TOSKA

TOSKA
Longings to Live

Narinder Kaur

PARTRIDGE

To order additional copies of this book, contact
Partridge India
000 800 10062 62
orders.india@partridgepublishing.com

www.partridgepublishing.com/india

Dedicated
To an unseen god
Watching my steps

To Bhavneet and Mankirat
The women who make life mystical

To Mandeep and Jaideep
The men who redefine love everyday

Why do we do this to ourselves
We the decorators of pain
Gouging our insides
And presenting them on a platter
Taking the ragged dolls of our beings
Patching it up with pretty words

Splattered on a corner of life
We the poets
Shaping our loves into sweet couplets
Shaping our lusts into sensuous songs

Why do we do this to us
Are we seeking fellow souls
Or filling up the voids of our selves
Our own words filling up
Our silences

~

Does God regret creating Man
Was it worth the effort
Wouldn't it have been better
To leave the earth to the animals and trees
Perhaps there would have been none
To appreciate the magnificent glory
Of Gods handiwork
At least there would have been none
To destroy and abuse
God's magnificent handiwork

Choose God
Do you want worship
Or
Do you want the earth

~

I have a way with words
I pick them
Choose them
Play with them
Savor them
Roll them in my gut
And put them side by side
I make love to my words
And explore

My words have a way with me
They invade me
Possess me
They get hold of me
And devour me
My words
They churn me
Push me around
Torture me
My words touch me
And explode.

~

A beautiful smile of a foggy day
Cold chilled gray
Misty like a dream
All further off lost to the vision
Only the immediate
Is alive

Like shrouded in the mists of love
Alive
Only to the moment of love
All else lost
To the gentle covers of faraway

Like shrouded in the patience of time
Still beautiful silent
Awaiting the sunshine
To rise and awake

~

Who will see the beautiful woman
High up on the roof
Mingling with the mists
The cold air flying in her hair
The chill coloring her cheeks
She is there
Playfully blowing soft mists
From her rounded lips
Her mists merging
With blowing fogs
She is smiling
With her whole being
Her love a mist
The mist her love
Beautiful illusive
Alluring
In the moment
Only hers to have
And treasure
In that sole lone place
Where she dwells
And her dreams

~

Have you ever felt
Hungry…

When a space hollows out
In the middle of your belly
And your throat
Is full of that emptiness
Every delicacy you have ever seen
Hovers in your eyes
Every juicy bit you have ever sucked
Sits on your tongue

So hungry
You will have any leftovers
The mouth waters
For every morsel
When everything is
A saucy juicy treat
Have you ever been…..
Hungry….

~

The plaid world of
Perfect relationships
The politeness of Sorry,
Thank you, please.
Putting the perfectly polished
Foot forward.
Putting up the nicer face
Being all accepting
All permissive.

The plaid world of perfect relationships.
Where flaws are kept
Nicely tucked away.
All things nice bloom and blossom
The weeds get no space.
Where the spadework
Is done in the dark.

Undemanding
Unsavoured

What will happen if this
Plaid world of perfect relationships
Comes in contact with
The psychedelic world of imperfect relationships.

Relationships
Where it's ok
To be stupid silly funny
Or wrong

Where it's ok
To demand and yell
Where you are your real
Authentic broken
Messed up being

Because that's you

Human imperfect flawed
Fat and gorgeous

The psychedelic world......

~

You don't have to be mine
To belong to me
There is so much of Me and You.
I can revel in you
Celebrate you
Have you
Yet not need to possess you

You can be mine
Like the breath in my body,
Yet with a life of its own.
You are mine
Yet not mine to keep.

How can it be.
When there is so much
That belongs to me
Yet isn't mine.
I can possess it
Yet not have it.

What is mine
Is a part of me, my life.
It makes me who I am.
Though it can never belong to me,
No one can take it from me.
That part that is mine forever.

~

The zaroori - ghair zaroori ilm of my soul.

How do I forsake it.

Even if I die
I cannot forsake it.

I could not forsake it
When I died.

Millions of times before.

Maybe,
Someday they will
Forsake me.

Then,
Perhaps I can die.

~

She wants to go
On a journey in her head.
She goes it all alone.
She goes and she knows not
Where she's going.
But oh, how she wants to go.
Wander and travel,
And get lost in the path.
And find herself again.

It hurts, this journey.
This wandering all alone.
But go she will for sure.

Just hold her warm body.
Feverish from travelling.
Till she tires and comes back home.

Will you do that.
Will you wait.
Will you hold on
And halt for her.

Is she worth it.
Will you want her.
When she's gone
And when she comes back.

~

I can't find my summer.
The winter has stretched out for so long
I can't find my sunshine,
The sun has been hidden for so long.
A chill has settled around my love.
Frozen cold, hunched over.
I sit curled in
Trying to warm myself.
Can't feel my limbs.
Can't feel my toes.
Can't feel my very skin.

The gray skies,
The white mists.
Surround me.
Drown me.

I remember,
A yellow sunshine,
A colorful spring.

I remember,
A very red
Flower of my garden.
Frozen in place.
Waiting ... awaiting.
My sunshine.

~

Why do you feel like a destination.
Like a tear drop
Lightening the heart.
The laughter of a friend.
The hug of a mother.
The sweet sleep of labor.

Why do you feel like a destination.
The word of truth.
The karma of all previous lives.
The last word of destiny.
The only word,
I want to…need to hear.

Why do you feel like a destination.
The lap I want to snuggle into.
Listening to my senseless whispers,
While I breathe in your essence
Digging my face in your chest.

How did you find me.
My destination.

~

The early morning bloom.
The untouched rose.
Holding all the dreams of the night
All the anticipation of the day.
Tender....budding.
Moist with the love of life.
Peeping out
The wild color
To the first rays of sunshine.
The tender lips
Parting.
The pink petals
Flourishing.
The fragrance bidding
Come hither.
Open to the first sight of
Dawn.

~

Talk to me.
Ask me.
Listen to me.
Explore me. My dear.

Wonder at me.
Wander within me.
Be curious.
You will find a wondrous being.
With bits and parts of you
Embedded in my soul.

I dare you
Come meet me
In the ethereal deeps of me.

Get entangled.
Be dazzled
Meet my shimmering web.

~

Constant consistent
A dripping tap in the background
Pervading everything
Riding on my skin
All the time
All over
Keeping out
All other thoughts and needs
Riding on my skin
Like little dots and dashes
Of a flashing signboard
Travelling fast
Emanating from
Reaching to
A thrumming throb
In the middle of my being

~

That moon lifeless, just reflecting the sun
With empty craters, not a whiff of breath
It sits there
Living, stinging under my skin.

Waxing and waning at its own free will
Now shining forth silver
Lighting up the cold night
Now a sliver
Of chopped up nights of delight.

Once it becomes a super moon
Glowing and fiery
Coming too close
Mimicking the source
Forgetting it's only a cold stone
Dizzying around a core.

Stinging under my skin
It plays with my tides
Taking me to Utopias
Dumping me into the Atlantis.

Oh, be my blue moon
And sting me to death
Come out of my skin
And sit on my breath...

~

A sharp cut
A sprinkle of tears.
That's how the earth is seeded
The seed of a thought
Drops into this valley
And covered back with
Disturbed soils.

Nurtured with pain.
With joys, with love,
With ecstasies, despairs.
A million forgotten memories.

The thought blooms.
Painfully shattering the seed.
Tearing apart the earth
Struggling to breathe
Gasping in the sunlight
Knowing not what it will be.

Sowed you some cacti
Some roses
Some orchids
I have now a garden full of thee.

~

Mystical blossoms Of poetic ecstasies.
Arising out of mysterious caverns.
Aroused...Alive...floating on breaths.
Each a vibration
Of a cosmic orgasm.
Each word each poem
A spasm of love.
The throes of erotic passions.
The poetic mystics The ecstatic blossoms.

Mystical ecstasies Of poetic blossoms.
Each word as it arises
Takes me beyond myself.
The ecstasy of birth
Captured in words of fantasy.
The pleasure the delight
Of finally beholding.
The mystical poems The blossoming ecstasies.

~

Woman.
How do you sleep alone.
In that great bed.
No man
No children
No home that were.
Do you fold the soft fluffy covers
To hug and hold at night.

Woman.
How do you sleep in that bed.
The man
The children
The home not yours.
The one to whom they belonged
Has left.
Do you feel a caretaker
More than a family.

Woman.
How do you sleep alone in the bed.
No man
No children
The home only yours.
Do you fill your empty spaces
With things.
And tell yourself
This is also life.

Woman.
How do you sleep at all.
The man
The children
The home
They have you.
Do you sleep in peace
Without yourself.

~

I like to see the bed unmade.
Every crevice in the bed sheet is a night of togetherness.
Not just lovemaking
But loving.
The careless abandon of being together
Like no one else you can be with.

The unmade people that wake up
Out of the unmade bed.
They unmade each other through the night.
Unmade the travels of the day.
Unmade the dust of the world settled on their beings.
Together they unmade each other
So they can face another day of life.

Unmade with a kiss….a hug
With a presence
With just being there.

~

So many words on paper
So much turmoil organized, dissected on paper.
So many hidden shades laid bare
Exposed to foreign eyes.

Yet there is so much more where that comes from.
So much that cannot be articulated.

Some thoughts need sounds
They need that hiccup in the throat
That pregnant pause
That says so much more than any string of words put
together.

That singular tone of voice
Only emotion of the core can evoke.

The gesture of hands
Trying to speak for me.

The touch of soft fingers
Speaking to your skin.

There is something to be read in my eyes
Only eyes present can read.

There is always more to be said
That cannot be put on paper.

~

I built myself in the womb
Gathered flesh and blood for my soul.
And then I was too much.
Expelled into light
My glue came off
Bits and parts of me came undone.

Now here I am
With gaping holes and crevices.

I go about the universe.
Looking for you
The one
Who can lend me some flesh.
Seeking someone with holes
Coordinating with mine.
So we can fit like a jigsaw puzzle
Perfectly.

Found.
Now I want you.
Want you like nothing else in destiny.
In return you have to want me too.
Together
We will take our wants
To a new destination.
Where we will grub out each other's holes.

But alas!
The man that you are

You filled your holes
And moved on.
Used me like a hole in the flesh
A hole of pleasures and desires.

You conveniently forget.
I am not a hole
I am completely
A soul.
A soul to create you
Complete you.

And if you have not the nerves to acknowledge
All I have to do
Is deny you my pieces.

To extinguish your existence forever
And dispense with my existence.

~

Don't leave me alone with my thoughts
It's a dangerous arena.
It's a deep thick forest in there
No sunlight streaming in
It's dark and damp.

You never know when I will be lost to you
Now, I will be surrounded
By a patch of lusty colored flowers
Happy and singing
Their aroma wafting all around me.

Now, I will step
Into a dark snake infested pit.
When sunlight patches
Will turn into dingy paths.

I cannot assure you.

I cannot assure you
When I will slip
From fiery to flighty to frisky.

Don't leave me alone with my thoughts
You will never know
What hit you
You will never know
Where to find me.

~

Moms

The vulnerable superheroes
Of our lives
As we move on
In the journey of motherhood
We realize everyday
Your journey

The early mornings
The late nights
The coordination of messes
The mistakes
That must have haunted you
The answers
You never really had
The questions
You never dared to ask
Your motherhood
Was your very personal
Very lonely
Learning experience

You still spread love
Strength and blessings

My motherhood
Is a continuation
Of your journey
Guide me always on this path
Love you Maa

~

You are gorgeous
When someone says that
It can be stunning
Breathtaking silencing
All at the same time
It is a moment
Of wonder
A moment that says
Beauty lies
In the eyes of the beholder

Beauty
A word
An association
When it relates
It is a moment of revelation
Reveling in the peace of being alive
To be beautiful is to be loved
To be loved
Is beautiful

~

I invite you
To feast on me

Join me

For a toast to insanity
The appetizers of my dreams
For starters I'll serve you my heart
The soup is a broth of lost words
Feast on the main course of my loves
We will wash it down
With the wines of my tears
Spice it up with my fears
Lets round it up with some smiles
For dessert you can have all my guile
With the night cap of a kiss
We shall depart
The feast is all on me
Oh my dear
You are, but, the star.

~

They ask me what do I do.
What I do for a living
What I do every day.

How do I explain.
I live for a living
I love for a living.

I live inside me
Making love to the insides.
I watch enthralled
As my insides
Reveal new universes.

Every day I wake up with new eyes
New suns shining on my sights
I see new vistas
New petals unfold.

And then,
Every day I pick up these visions
I travel through my vocabulary
The fragile load of my visions
Selecting the words
To capture these vistas
Before they dissipate…evaporate

Tell me
Isn't this living.

~

I talk myself through my life
Telling
Instructing
Berating
Scolding
Cajoling
Myself through tasks.

I walk myself through my life
Watching my steps
Jumping the gaps
Stepping on pebbles
Rushing through rapids
Stumbling
Falling
Still moving
Trying to reach somewhere

Its dark and its silent
My own voice echoes
And scares me
My steps falter
My core and balance
Destabilized
My life
My journey
My mess.

~

As I put pen to paper
It's an infinity loop
Completed
I fill the paper
The paper fills me

As I put forth myself
In ink
I am real.

~

This is the night
The night you have chosen
To not take her.

Tonight her skin is alive
Every cell of her
So alive.

The touch of your sleeping hand
Gives her more than just goose bumps
Your sleeping breaths
Are weaving inside her.

Her breath is fragrant
With a special desire.
She has it wafting all around
She has special ambers
Igniting her lips
Special embers
They are within.

She has special churnings
Whirling within

All this
And she is prepared

A special night
You have chosen
To leave her beautiful
And unhad

~

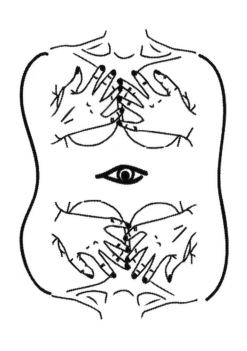

The half taken woman
With half tamed storms
In her belly
Half hearted half willing
Her stars half shining

A brewing storm
A tornado half twisted
A core half done
Half undone

Half the woman
Still to be unleashed
Half the love
Untasted

Till she meets
Again
With her half
She leaves her half
To you

~

Sometimes up here
I feel a fluttering
My heart whispers to my head
Come let's run away
Elope with me
Let's go somewhere else
Let's fly
Let's plant us anew
Let's grow a new garden
This place had its glory
It was good
Come, let's move on

~

I don't remember why I first fell in love with you
The memory holds no ground
The falling doesn't matter

All that remains is the love
A simple spontaneous trickle of a glow
A breath like substance
That permeates and pervades me

And now I can do nothing else
But love
You

~

There is a dance
Captured within me
A movement
Rare and beautiful
There is a flow
I feel flowing
A rhyme A rhythm
Of my own

It is closed and captured
Somewhere deep

It keeps whirling
In a deep vacuum

It just doesn't
Reach my limbs
It just doesn't
Break through

I am looking
For that music
The song
That will
Lift me

Make me sway
To My rhythm
To the sunshine
To my heart's content

~

We began as friends
Laughing together into eyes of youth
Together we found
The first crevices of love
Hidden in lovemaking

Together we moved
Now close now far

Together we kept
The love at par

The Journey has been long
The love has been battered
Still together
We keep on the walk

The love we will keep
Sheltered in bosoms
The journey is long
Love is all we will need

~

They say there is too much of me
I need to trim myself
Drop a pound here
A curve there
Cut yourself to shape
So you can fit into ready-mades

I say there is so much of me
A luscious curve here
A huggable swell there
I don't fit in factory mades
I go for customized

Yes there is plenty of me
I am a substantial woman
A woman of substance

~

Translate me
To a more comprehensible language
A language more comprehensible to you
Translate my foreignness
To something closer home

But beware
If you dare
To translate me

You have to be
A master
Of my language
And yours

I give you permission
For translation
Not transcriptions
No interpretations

Translate me
As I am
Word for word

~

You are the prism
Dispersing me
Into a dazzling multicolored glow
You catch hold of me
And I am no longer
Just a shaft
Of blinding white light

You are the mist
Spreading me into a rainbow
All you need
Is a sliver of me
And even a gray day
Will smile
Into a crayon box
Full of hues

~

A maroon silk
Dark deep shining
Like the first bloods
Rich luxuriant
Spreading around my waist

Black fur
Warm ensconcing
Soft
Purring round my face

White lace
Shining enticing
Falling softly
Round my fingers

Blue velvet
Luxuriant shimmering
Slithering down
My bosom

Purple wine
Tall glass
Dripping down
My lips

~

Travelling lights
Interspersed with the night
Flashes of forbidden thoughts
Brightening the dark skies
Of a tiring journey
The comfortable enclosure
Carrying me to predestined destination
All I have to do is
Allow myself to be carried

My thoughts rushing ahead of me
Weaving webs through my silences

Enveloped in the bright darkness
The song that drifts up to me
Carries me away
To where I belong

~

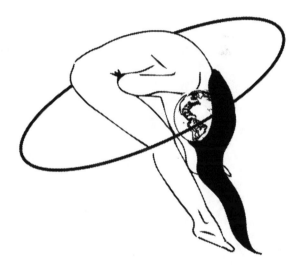

Dreams desire
Stars universe
Futile
Dreams mere sleep sojourns
Desires expectations of the flesh
Stars mere holes in the night sky
The universe just a place to be
The futility of this existence
Enhanced by indifference

~

How can I allow myself to be misused
I am not a little trinket
Sitting pretty on a velvet bed
Awaiting lusting fingers or adoring eyes

I am a person
Full and complete
Full of lusts and desires
Complete with loves and wants

Why do I await you
Have you made yourself
Worth my while

Be worthy of my desires
Deserve my longing
Rise up to my loves
Be a worthy suitor

I am not subject to availability
I am an object of desire

~

So fragile
So futile
What are we
But a cosmic joke
A couple of breaths
A rotting flesh
A flash in the pan

So finite
So miniscule
Our plans
So comically grand

Memories
We seek
To create
For a legacy

Deeds and actions
To impress upon lives

I hope it was all
Worth it

~

My cocoon
Encasing me
I spit out my own silk
Weave my own cage

My cocoon
The cocoon in the butterfly
Flying frittering beautiful butterfly
With its own cocoon inside

Getting denser tighter
With every flight
The larva inside
Choking on its own bulk

Some day
This whole package will burst
Butterfly cocoon larva
You will find them splattered
On the road side

~

I am not yet complete
I am not yet ready to share myself

I have a calcified centre
No pyre can burn this bone
No coffin can consume it

I am running out of time on this earth
And I have not reached the marrow yet

My vocabulary has not reached
The capacity of my depth
My words have not sorted me

My silence has not found me
My screams have not drowned me

I yet have my I
I yet have to lose myself

I still generate warmth
I have yet to ignite a fire

~

Some days the muse doesn't show up
The inspiration is just not in working order
The words sit silent
Grouchy in the corner
Refusing to rouse
Grouchy …a little sad
Groping, teary eyed

Show some sunlight
Let these words bloom
Let them flow in melody
Let them dance their tune

They will sing a song
Dance their dance
Maybe a little off beat
Till the muse turns up

~

The days when prayers come
To my lips
Come unbidden
Inspite of myself

The days when no hope is visible
Not even in the prayer
Yet the prayer comes to my lips

When the prayer is my only solace
Thinking of the actual problem
Is a futile exercise in pain

The days when shamefacedly I pray
Not even knowing what to pray for

~

Soft
The feather in her hair
Soft
The thought on her cheek
Soft
The whisper in her eye

The breeze in her words
Soft
The halt in her breast
Soft
The wait in her breath
Soft

~

I am the goddess
`Mother earth
Part land part water

The peopled land
It grows on my breast
Digging its roots into my being
Crawling up my throat
Choking me
Growing inside outside my head
Taking me over

Below I am all water
Swirls currents
Churning the skin on my belly
Waves upon waves
Thrashing upon me
Oceans free flowing
Numerous
Making up the rest of me
Alive with strange exotic lives
Lives colorful
Of emotions and desires
Storming me
Responding to my moon
And the sun

How strange
The 1/4th land controls all of me
Polluting ruling

Creating destroying
My destiny

And all of 3/4th of me
Is ignored
Left to fend for itself
It's lashing storms
Not paid heed to

Till it smashes crazy
Tsunamis on the shore
Till it destroys displaces
Those arrogant ignorant people

~

Ouch
It hurts
The leaving
The repetition still doesn't
Blunt the blow
Day in and day out
It happens again and again
Yet
It hurts
The leaving

As we go our ways
Taking life by the horns
Utilizing the day
We leave behind our shadows
Clutching hands in the bed

Looking forward
To coming back in the evening
And slipping back into the shadows

Till then do we part
Do we hurt
Ouch

~

The derriere of a desire
Walking ahead of me
Tantalizingly out of reach
I glance at her longingly
Swaying hypnotically
Glancing over her shoulder

This gorgeous desire
She won't wait or halt
There she is
Always a few steps ahead

I follow mesmerized
Now stunned to a pause
Now rushing to catch up

The desire
Her curves, inviting a caress
Voluptuous and hungry

Someday
Get hold of this desire
And kiss her full on the mouth

~

All I want is a corner of your chest
To rest my cheek
All I want is a nook of your arm
To surrender my soul

All I want is the sound of your heartbeat
To lull me to sleep

All I want is the feel of your breath
To keep me alive

Is it too much to ask

Just your fingers on my hand

Your eyes on my smile

Just your voice
To say that you care

All I want is a bit of you
To call my own
So I can give my all to you

~

Tortured souls of this world
Unite over dregs of leftover
Poetry
Toasting their wounds
Cheers to the pains of this world
Bottoms up with the vials
Of the hearts blood
Down them with bottles of vodka
Let them drown in their own silly shots
Let them be the tequilas

~

Still there was something left of me

Something unrealized
Unknown
Some part of destiny
Held a secret treasure of me
A secret withheld even from me
A secret to be explored
Discovered
To dazzle me with myself
When my life was down and out

~

The woman with a million senses
Half a million of them unexplored

Yes she can deceive herself
For it is not deception
It is the flowering of
A few thousand more senses

Oh how can you say
Her reality is complete
When half a million senses
Lie hidden in her universe

She will never be explored
All in this life

You will never be enough
To explore her all

~

Drunk with passion
The clouds
Thick heavy loaded
Climb down into the valley
Entering forbidden depths
The clouds
They belong high up there
The valley
Forever empty here
What business do they have
Coming together
But it happens
Once the clouds are too full
They have to come
Into their beloved valley
Raining their bounties
Over the beauteous valley
Lightened of their burdens
The clouds disperse
To meet again

~

The weeping wailing walls
The ones in the middle of the tunnel
Weeping
Dark and wet
The walls that will never see sunshine
Always dank with seeping moisture
Screaming their anguish
As the train shoots through
The train loaded with life
The train rushing towards sunlight
Wailing loudest in the middle
The darkest deepest spot
Screaming
Forever grounded

Be the train
Forever rushing through every darkness
The tunnels of pain shall be many in life

~

The ocean rages tormented
The depths screaming in anguish
Churning
Foaming
Forcing mighty waves
Higher thicker
They rush on and on
Seeking, who knows what sky
They rush and thrust
Wild with desire
Rising out of the oceans guts

Crashing on the shores
Going all silent
Kissing the shore
Going all love
Meeting the sands
And going all stars

The waves are all about meeting the shore.

~

I want someone to follow me with a camera
And capture all my faces
I want him to make me laugh
Cry think talk run jump fly
And flop down on the ground
I want him to want to pic me
In every mood and mode
I want to see myself as he sees me
I want to pose and flutter
And flirt with the shutter
I want to be your muse
And amuse you

~

The sun shines everyday
Sustaining
Maintaining life
Keeping the earth warm and blooming
Constantly consistently
Unrelentingly
Uncomplainingly

Yet the oceans
Move with the moon
The rock of borrowed lights
The dweller of darkness
Inconsistent
Waxing and waning

What is the pull
Of this fickle fellow
That keeps the ocean
Swelling beauteously

~

I see you waiting for me
To arrive
How long have you been waiting
Has it been forever and ever
How did it happen
That I went asunder
Where is it that
I am coming back from
Why did you let me go
Why didn't you come with me
How long will it be
Till I arrive
I have been gone for long
Will I arrive this time
Or will we have to travel
All the more
I see you
So far
Waiting for me
Arrive, how,
Perhaps this time
I will

~

The upside down heart
The one that defies gravity
My topsy-turvy heart
Won't let me stay below
You see
Its sight is set on the stars

My blood won't stay within
It gushes out of my eyes

My upside down heart is pouring
My upside down heart is open
It's open at the wrong end

It forgets to be a heart
And turns into a fountain

My topsy-turvy heart
Trippy traipsing all over
My silly little hearts gone turtle
Don't ever turn it right again

~

Wedded to a commitment
A commitment to adore your flaws
To envy your qualities
A commitment to follow your responsibilities
To enjoy your comforts

Committing to let you fly
When you need air
To catch you close
Before you fall

A commitment to cherish your touch
To breathe your air
To glorify in the sight of your beauty
To see the prettiness in your quirky ways

To know how, where and why you hurt
To forgive you for your lousy ways

A wedding is not the commitment
The commitment is the wedding
The wedding of love
And its infinite possibilities

~

It's not a need
It's a want
There's a difference

Needs have reasons
Purposes
Pros and cons.
Needs have justifications
They are means to an end
Needs are tasks.

Wants
Are desires
Unjustified
Unreasonable
Purpose, be damned
Wants defy logic
Wants drive crazy
Wants are life

Needs are goals

Wants are ambition

~

I am entangled in you
Torn battered
Bruised and bleeding

I am the fluttering strip
Of a fiery red dupatta
Flying desperately
In the winds of your desire
Forever caught
Faded to a dirty shade
In the tortuous sunshine of your wait

There is a piece of my flesh
Caught in you
The dried blood
The rotting vessels
A piece of breast
Torn when I tried to cross you

You are my barbed wire
Separating me from my reality

There are vistas beyond you
I can see

I can't reach there
Till I cross you

I won't cross you
And I won't stay

You won't come with me
And you won't let me go

I am entangled in you
Caught in the beautiful
Ribbons of your being

Entangled in you
I can't go on in my life
Without you
I don't want to

~

My mirror My therapist
My personal diary
My mirror
Not the standing shiny stiff kind
My mirror is the clearest of lakes
Shining
In the clearest sunshine
Reflecting me truly
No judgments No advice

Reflecting my beauty in its own
Rippling with my tears
Laughing with my breath
Always blowing me cool breezes
Drenching me with love

My mirror lets me swim
In its cool therapeutic waters
Lets me swim stark naked
Naked of inhibitions
Naked of prohibitions

~

I have found a new place to exist.
I now reside in my gut.
There around my navel you can find me.
There I reside in the form of a storm.
There I am a distant galaxy of numerous stars and
worlds.
I exist in my black holes and satellites.

The air I breathe finds its way to my depths.

From there I come forth
The shining stars of my skin.
The silent words of my lips.
The streaming drops of my eyes.

You can find them all coming from there.

If you want to meet me
You can always find me there.
Just knock on my smiles with a kiss.

~

You bring everything together
The rainbow and the stars
The words and the stories
The deeps and the highs

You bring it all so close
The smiles and the blush
The lips and the smile
The courage and the action

You place them side by side
The gorgeous and the beautiful
The seductive and the attractive
The body and the soul

You bring everything together
The essence
The intoxication
The hangover

~

Give her a thread
She will weave you a tapestry
Give her a word
She will tell you a story
Give her a drop
She will drench you in her oceans
Give her a thought
She will give you all her loves
Give her a smile
She will fill you with bliss
Give her a glance
She will show you her universe
Give her your love
She will give you her life

The woman of fine sensibilities.

~

I know that feeling
I know it only too well
That feeling
When the consent
Is not entirely mutual
When a yes is met
By a no
When I ask with my reality
You reply with yours

That feeling
When my abundance passes by you
You
Already full
Already taken

When we meet halfway
And you are already gone

I know that feeling
And I know
How to live with it.

~

The punctuation and the dots
A comma here
Bidding you to halt
A full stop saying
It's done
A capital letter saying
Look at me
An ellipses…..taking you there

The assistants of conveyance

The words are roads
Long winding
Going on and on
From here to there
From nowhere to everywhere

The punctuations
Make these roads a journey
A turn A bend
The red light The curve

The destination The reaching
The meaning….My words.

~

Unleash the child woman
The raw emotion
The curiosity. The sensitivity.
The rare simple awareness.
The unabashed longing
The reckless boldness
All unleashed
The child woman
She still has some naiveté.
Still wondrous. Still curious.
Amazed yet delighted
Open
Welcoming every experience with a throaty giggle
She laughs She sings
She dances She skips
Happy to be found
The child woman
Unleashed upon a world

~

Go slow
Take care
This is a luxury
It is caviar
You don't gobble it
You don't gorge
This is a delicacy...so rare
Procured with dangers
A labor of love
Special occasions
A special day
The rare aroma
The indulgent flavor
The gorgeous texture
The exotic sight
The beauty lies in the rarity
This is a luxury
The caviar of life

~

High up in the ivory tower
Rapunzel
An ocean of tresses growing
Out of her head
Golden, abundant, beautiful.
She stays inside the tower
Combing, caressing, braiding
Her ever growing hair.

The magical locks
They are all her world
She is happy in her tower
Only her tresses for company.

Her tresses are her ladder
To the world without.

The prince climbs her locks
And leaves there in
There is no other doorway
No steps up the cave.

She never realizes
So lost she was
Her Rapunzel tresses
When they turn to Medusa
Making her frightful
Freezing all around her

Her magic mirror
Showing her only her golden tresses.

Rapunzel in her tower
Nourishing her golden tresses

And me in my towers
With my Rapunzel thoughts
Growing out of my head…..

~

Take me with you
I want a doomed love
Take me and hold me close
Close enclosed
Wrap me in the mesh of your being
Hold me
Embrace
Fit me into your nooks
Rising and dropping
Breathe for me
While I still
These storms within

Take me
Let's doom this love
Doomed since inception
Doomed till eternity
Doom this love
To forever anticipation
Doomed to forever separation

Doom this love
Bury it in the earth of my chest

If ever there is life beyond
We will take this doomed love
And see its blooms sprinkling
My earth and your sky.

~

Beloved
I have to go
Let me untangle my limbs
Give me my fingers
My legs I will need
Take your breath out of my hair

Let go of my bosom
Free my waist
Here let me kiss you
It's not a goodbye

The sun is up
The day is peeping in
Life is await
The lights are creeping in

Let's go say hello
To people all around

I'll see you again
Till then
Let me have my eyes.

~

Stories.
Superimposed experiences
On fictional characters
Blending the horizons
Of reality and unreal
Digging into forgotten tales
Looking for unseen parables
Hunting the scenes
Missed in the first go
Finding ways and means
To unearth life
Out of the everyday humdrum
Searching the memorable moments

Or flying with a very flighty imagination

Creating characters and incidents
Step by step
Out of thin air
Stories
The legends of a life.

~

My skin
The largest organ of my body
Is just a cover up for a starry universe

There are meteors of feelings shooting across
Feelings that flare up now and then
Shoot across and burn themselves
Burning off their own intensity and speed

There are twinkling stars
Thoughts long gone
Far away
I can never capture them
Only watch them from here
And marvel
At their alien brightness

There are black holes too
The dark thoughts
I dare not venture into
They will suck up my entire being
And no one will ever know
Where I went

There is a bright burning sun
Too hot to handle
Sustaining the life inside me
Sustaining the steady planets of love
That make up my life

The numerous colorful
Fascinating galaxies
Beckoning me
To explore
Their beauty beyond comprehension

The universe inside me
I hide it all under my skin

I wonder
If you have the eyes
To see the stars
Shooting out of my skin

Now and then.

~

So heavy to carry you within
You came with your seeds
Magnanimous and magnificent
The seeds of your awakened powers
The seeds of lifetimes of fruition

Raising me to an ecstasy
You placed your seeds within me
In my empty shells

My empty shells
Empty…spent
Some yet to be taken

Your seed placed
You have left now

I carry you within
I am full with you
Heavy
With you

You sit inside
Growing
Feeding on my being
Corroding me on miniscule levels

Outward
I am glowing
With a new life

Inside
I am bloated
Choking on the very air I breathe

No, this is not how it was supposed to be
This was a journey
Of growth and abundance
Of moving on and forward

Then why this chill and stillness
Why this abandoned feel

This seed will grow to fruition
Will grow to a glowing oak

Till then I carry you
Within me
Heavy with you
My love.

~

I wish to move now
Move
Beyond you
And reach myself

I wish to see
Myself
See as I feel myself
Feel as I behold myself

The self I carry
As a burning torch
Illuminating all around me

I want to stare
Into that glow
Burn my eyes
With fiery colors

Its time I met me
And reveled in the company.

~

Let her rave and rant
Let her speak her mind
Unburden her soul
Let her go on

Like a clock work toy
She is all wound up
Once the key is wound tight
You
Can't stop her

She will whir and whirl
And then her key will unwind
And she will slowly purr to a stop

Nice and quiet
She will become the pretty
Again.

~

Few words
Are worth days
Worth days of longing
And waiting
Days of putrefying in the belly

Worth days of holding on
Till the next few words

Few words
Are worth days
The rest fall along the sides
Few words
They continue to cling
To the web of the soul

~

Your fingers
As they weave across my body
Exciting nerves
I never knew I had
Your fingers of fire
Leaving stars on my skin
They know
Where they need to go

It's not that your fingers
Are good with anatomy
It's not that they know
Every crevice and technique

It's the weaving they do
Of the web to my soul
The thread they bring
From your being

Your fingers
They know me
We are made of one skin
The nerves they begin in you
The endings within me

Of course
You excite me
How else can it be

For you and me
Are meant to be

~

The sliver of sunshine
Slashed through
The dark clouds
Kissing the forehead
Of the mighty rock

The waves wrapping
Around her
Exploring the curves
The crevices
Of the island

The breeze patting
Her forests
The favorite sound
Of her body

Kissing whispering
The ocean takes
Her all
Over and over
Again.

~

What do I do
With the silence and loneliness
Settling inside my centre
It is homing in there
A beautiful silk web
Is whirling around my insides
Slowly diligently
Wrapping me up
A gift for whom

There is white snow within
Softly covering
All my innerscape
Beautiful
And chilling
Happily freezing and numbing me
To the life around me.

~

Hush my dear
Don't get into
The how why when and where
Just float on your senses

Let the breeze carry you
Feel your breath
Keep you alive
Smell around you the love

Not the color
But the thought within
Will carry you
Far and beyond
Set your sights
On the rainbow
The dust storms are
But a distraction.

~

Mother by day
Girl by night
Wherefore the woman

I glimpse her sometimes
In the mirror
In seeking eyes
In flowing tresses
Within the luxurious bosom

I peek her at times
In the pride of her gender
In the centuries
Of living up to herself

She is still there
Evolving
She knows it

Well preserved
And groomed

One day
She will be
All woman
That day the world
Will meet the moon.

~

Beautiful words
Descriptions heartfelt
Words dripping from the soul

The bees of the sunlight
Gather this nectar
From a myriad hued flowers

The flowers blooming
In the garden of life
Watered with love
Planted in pain
Breathing the air of pleasures

Dripping honey of words
Garnished with crystals
Of appreciation.

~

I lost my soul
In the heart of you
Will you search and find it

Find it and see
If its dead or alive
Bruised, battered or blinded
Find it and tell me
If you will have it
Keep it close and safe

Find it
Tell me
If I can have it back
For I need a soul to live
Find me mine
Or let me have
Yours.

~

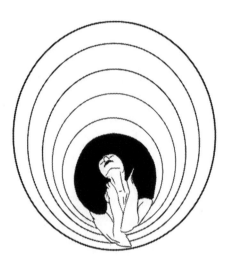

Stealing myself
From the stars of my destiny
Spangling up all fancy

Stealing myself
For purposes of my own
For reckless purposes
For living purposes

Desperate measures
When I have to steal
Myself
From my destiny.

~

Love him
Like you walk a tightrope
Living each foothold
Balancing every breath
Keep that high strung tension
It will keep you alive
And high up there

Love him
Like you walk a beach
Let the sands rich
Squish through your toes
Let the sands blow
Into every curve and crevice of your body
Walk along the beach
Let him spread himself like the ocean
And get dizzy
Within the still sands
And crashing waves of his love

Love him
Like you walk a forest
Feel the breeze
Ruffle your hair
The flowers kiss your eyes
Feel the earth
Hold and caress you
Feel the life walking beside

Love him
Like you walk by him
Hand in hand
Sometimes quiet
Love him.
Just.

~

It's beautiful when you find someone
In love with your mind
In love with the idea of you
In love with being a part of your thought process
Someone attracted to your seduction
Someone seduced by your attraction
Someone that wants to undress your conscience
And make love to your thoughts
To caress your hidden recesses
And kiss the curves of your soul
To rub the joys into your being
To lick away the fears

Someone whispering the sounds of courage
Going deep into the oceans of your eyes
Someone who wants to explode into your life
Molding you into the folds of his abundance

It's beautiful
With someone
In love with
You.

~

Take me to the edge of a cliff
And tip me off
Say goodbye
To a receding me
Flying down the steep walls

Floating away with the chill winds
Aimless
Weightless
My eyes one with the sky
My breath on a bird's wing

Slowly Gently
I will go away

You don't have to see
My being

Splattered
On the rock bottom.

~

Sitting with my feelings
Lying beside my emotions
Tasting the presence
Relishing the being
Touching tentatively
Feeling the pulsations
Scorching in the heat
The whispering desires

Feelings and emotions
Filled rich expanding
Emotions and feelings
Dripping with anticipation
Ravenous for fulfillment
Waiting
Awaiting

~

Be my sky
And always be there
The sky
Large blue expansive

Be my sky
And I shall be
The soft cotton clouds
The bright sunlight
The fresh morning
The twinkling twilight
The outrageous storm

I will be
The richly colored evening
The starry night

Be my sky
The singular, stable canvas
For the largeness
The manyness
That is me

Be my sky
For without you
I cannot be.

~

Empty depleted
A deep disturbing void
Do you know what happens
When you are empty inside.
Anyone can get inside you
And make you do
What they want
You react
You behave in spite of yourself
Without a sense of self
A hypnotized puppet
Of the surfaces
Then
Everything they say
Is personal
A personal assault
Their emotions
Their needs
Their perceptions
You acting them out

The empty vessel
Echoing empty winds.

~

Don't

Don't try to extract me
Don't try to explore me
Don't try to bring out the real me
I am a dangerous person
I question
I question everything
I can go on and on
With my questions
I can be blasphemous
I don't really believe in anything
I don't have any opinions
I refuse to settle on any
I will find fault with everything
Everything has the other side
And that other side fascinates me
Leave me alone with my doubts
I will talk to myself
And reach no where
Get exhausted with my journey
And come back
Let me be as I am
And I will be here

~

Where do you keep
The layers of you
When all that is required
Is the cover

Hide them in a closet
Or tuck them in tight
Gag their mouth
Bind the limbs
Lest they peek out to the sunshine

A cover
Is all we need to live
A cover
Is all that life requires
And can bear.

~

There are still worlds
To be travelled
Universes to be traversed
Still reasons to be explored
Still questions to be answered
Still everything
Does not make sense
Still everything
Is yet to be justified

Yet it is all
Perfect.

~

Printed in the United States
By Bookmasters